THE BEST OF NATURE'S HEALTH FOODS

A revealing guide to some health-giving food supplements which are essential additions to the modern, denatured diet.

By the same author

NATURAL COLD CURES
(*with Maurice Hanssen*)

THE BEST OF NATURE'S HEALTH FOODS

The Richest Sources of Natural Nutrition

by

JACK EDEN

Illustrations by Ray Barnett

NATURE'S WAY

THORSONS PUBLISHERS LIMITED
Wellingborough, Northamptonshire

First published 1979

ISBN 0 7225 0568 X

Photoset by Specialised Offset Services Ltd, Liverpool and printed and bound in Great Britain by Weatherby Woolnough Ltd, Wellingborough Northamptonshire

CONTENTS

INTRODUCTION

This book talks principally about twelve specific foods or supplements each of which has a particular use or uses in maintaining good health. But none of these will work to proper effect unless it is coupled with a diet that is balanced and made up of natural foods that still contain all their nutrients.

There has been a lot of talk about nutrition and diet over the past few years; so much so, in fact, that a common reaction has been to ask: 'What *is* all this? Our forefathers never bothered about all these fads and fancies and they seemed to survive and were probably a lot healthier than we are.' This is true enough in many ways, but our forefathers didn't have to worry about their food to the same extent because it came with all its nutrients intact anyway.

It is only in these days of mass production, refining and packaging into neat convenience food packs, that we have to stop and ask ourselves: 'What really is in this packet, or loaf of bread, or bag of sugar?' Life for many people these days is both hectic and sedentary, too – both stress-filled and lacking in the proper relaxation and exercise the body needs to keep in peak condition.

DENATURED FOODS

Today, the bread we eat, if it is white, contains little more than starch; sugar is purely sucrose, which is bad for the teeth, and most packaged foods have undesirable additives to give them colour, flavour, or whatever the manufacturer chooses to tempt the buyer with. These arguments may sound as though they have been around for a long time, and so they have, but the fact remains that food which should just be the pure and natural food we are entitled to enjoy is sold as 'health' food because the bulk of what is available on supermarket shelves is the denatured type.

Basically, we need a range of nutrients, in the right balance, to keep us fit and well. We need vitamins and minerals, as well as fats, carbohydrates, and protein, which are the energy foods. But too much carbohydrate or fat, or the wrong sort of fat, or food that is just a mass of carbohydrate without accompanying vitamins and minerals, puts the diet out of balance and a multitude of problems arise.

VITAMINS

Vitamins are broken down into several types: The main ones are vitamin A, the B complex, C, D, E, K, and P. Vitamin A is not one that usually causes problems as it is present in most foods, particularly green vegetables and fish oil. It is necessary for good eyesight, and for healthy skin and mucous membranes.

The vitamin B complex is made up of at least nine different vitamins that we know something about. Vitamin B_1 (thiamin or aneurin) has to be taken in sufficient quantities every day as it cannot be stored in the body. This is not difficult with a balanced diet, as it is contained in green vegetables, dairy produce, meat, soyabeans, yeast and wheat germ. Thiamin is needed for good muscle tone and for the nervous system. It is particularly important for the heart and intestinal muscles.

Vitamin B_2 (riboflavin), which again is important for the nervous system, as well as the eyes and skin, is found in green vegetables, peanuts, soyabeans, molasses, dairy produce, meat, yeast, and wheat germ. Another vitamin for the nervous system, nicotinic acid (niacin), the anti-pellagra vitamin, is found in wholegrains, yeast, molasses, milk, and liver. Lack of this causes headaches and digestive disorders.

Pyridoxine (B_6) is a tonic vitamin, essential for general good health and the metabolism of proteins. It is found in wheat germ, fruit, fish, yeast, and some green vegetables. Another tonic vitamin is B_{12} and a deficiency of this causes anaemia.

Biotin is an antiseptic which is needed for proper growth, so that a deficiency causes skin complaints and muscle pain, as well as general lassitude. It is found in vegetables, nuts, molasses, and liver.

Vitamin B_3 (pantothenic acid) is thought to give extra vitality and a longer life, and also to prevent greying hair. A deficiency, however, does not just mean that these advantages are curtailed, for it brings on dizziness and constipation as immediate symptoms. This vitamin is found in eggs, molasses, yeast, liver, and wholegrains.

Folic acid, another growth vitamin, is found in yeast, liver and green vegetables, while the fat-dissolving vitamins, Choline and Inositol, are in wholegrains and meat.

Vitamin C (ascorbic acid) has come to the forefront because of its ability to prevent colds if taken in large enough quantities. The body cannot store C, so it must be taken every day – and every day in large doses if a cold seems imminent. Apart from cold prevention, it is necessary for the bones, cartilage and teeth, and helps the body to get rid of toxic substances. The main sources of vitamin C are fruit, particularly citrus fruit, and vegetables, though it is also found in other foods, such as honey, in lesser amounts.

Vitamin D, which is found in green vegetables, fish, oils, liver, and dairy produce, is important for bone formation and as a preventive against bone disease, as well as having an effect on the thyroid gland, and the rate at which the cells use other foods.

Vitamin E, a muscle toner important for the prevention of nervous disorders, heart disorders, anaemia, and sometimes sterility, is found in wheat germ, eggs, milk, seed oils, and green vegetables.

Vitamin K, found in green vegetables, vegetable oils, liver, tomatoes, and soya, is essential for the clotting of the blood. Vitamin P, which is needed for healthy capillaries, is found in citrus fruits.

From this brief summary of the vitamins, what they do for you and where they are found, it can be seen that a balanced diet will give supplies of them all. A balanced diet being one that is full of plenty of green vegetables, (eaten raw for preference) wholegrains and fruits, as well as the other individual items mentioned.

ESSENTIAL MINERALS

Minerals are found in the soil initially, and therefore form part of any food which grows, and that includes most food in one way or another, except those that have been denatured and synthesized. Fruit and vegetables are the most ready source of minerals generally, but the precise amount of mineral salt in any one food varies depending on the type of soil it was grown in, how long it was grown for, which part of the world it was grown in, climatic conditions, and so on. This is why organically-grown foods are said to have a higher mineral content than those where the soil has been made inferior by artificial fertilizers; organic composting puts everything back into the soil and keeps it rich, whilst the artificial variety tends to reduce the quality of the soil over a period.

It is important that the diet contains enough minerals in the right proportion because they do not necessarily operate as individual elements, but interact with each other. If you do not think that your diet is very high in mineral content, you can take a daily supplement of minerals, either in the form of one of the mineral foods discussed in this book, or in tablet form.

The important salts from a nutritional point of view number about twenty, of which some are required only in tiny quantities, while others, such as calcium and iron, are needed in large amounts.

Calcium, potassium and sodium are all necessary for muscle tone, and also strengthen bones and teeth. Potassium is itself a very important mineral, not only for muscles, but also for nerve stability and digestive and intestinal disorders. Sodium is the mineral that gives a salty taste to perspiration and is excreted through the kidneys and the skin. It should therefore be replaced often in hot conditions where the skin is sweating heavily, since its presence prevents the formation of gall stones and kidney stones, as well as being allied to calcium and potassium.

Phosphorus is also allied to calcium for strong bone formation, but in addition to this function, it metabolizes carbohydrates, proteins and fats, and converts sugar into energy. Another important factor is that it keeps the acid/alkali balance of the blood stable and is important for the nervous system. Magnesium also helps the action of calcium, but is a laxative and diuretic too. Sulphur is a tonic which helps the liver to assimilate the other minerals and also to secrete bile. It cleanses the bloodstream, and helps to clear up skin disorders.

Chlorine also acts on the liver, as well as helping to get rid of waste products from the body and keeping the joints supple.

Iron is the mineral that most people have heard of, because it is so important for rich, pure blood. Iron builds haemoglobin, essential for the blood, and a deficiency causes anaemia. It is a particularly important mineral for women who lose a lot of blood during menstruation. Copper helps the iron to build up haemoglobin and is therefore also associated with red blood and anaemia, though it is not needed in such large quantities as iron. Another mineral connected with anaemia is cobalt, because it forms a proportion of vitamin B_{12}.

Manganese is an important mineral for the nerves and is also allied to iron in the red blood cells. Iodine, the main source of which is seaweed, is essential for the thyroid gland, and a deficiency can cause goitre and obesity.

Fluorine is often heard of in connection with teeth because it prevents dental caries. It is normally assimilated from water where it is present in the form of fluoride, but where the fluoride is excessive, hardening of the arteries can occur. So, unless the balance is right, fluorine can have mixed blessings, and it is better if the teeth are kept healthy through eating the right sorts of food.

OTHER ESSENTIAL NUTRIENTS

The other nutritional requirements are amino acids, protein, fats, and carbohydrates. Amino acids are needed for the repair and renewal of cells and tissues, and since they are introduced as a result of the digestion of protein, they are obviously mainly contained in the protein foods: meat, fish, dairy produce, and nuts. On the other hand, a diet heavy in meat protein can become too acid, and it is important to ensure that the acid/alkali balance is kept right. Fruit and vegetables are alkali foods, so that the best source of amino acids is the vegetable one – soya, seed oils, wheat germ, pulses, and so on, although meat need not be cut out altogether.

Acid foods other than meat are fats, refined foods, and stimulants such as tea and coffee. The diet should concentrate on fruit and vegetables and non-acid proteins, keeping the acid foods down so that the correct balance is maintained. Minerals also help to neutralize excess acid.

The carbohydrates are of course the starch foods such as bread and sugar and are needed for energy. However, refined foods produce starch only, without the accompanying nutrients which come with wholewheat flour or raw sugar, or molasses. Fats are also necessary in the diet, but these should be kept as far as possible to vegetable fats – seed and vegetable oils rather than lard, unsaturated margarine rather than butter, not too much meat.

It is obvious that to suggest a diet wholly devoid of any refined or non-organically grown food is not practical for most people. Sometimes all the ingredients of a product and their sources may not be known; or people may wish to eat meat at least for some of the time. A balance must be struck between the ideal, the cost, and convenience, of course, but most people can at least introduce plenty of fruit, vegetables and salads into their meals, and there are signs that there is a switch in favour of the more tasty wholewheat bread anyhow. Natural sweeteners – raw sugar, molasses, honey – can easily be taken in place of white sugar, and all this lays the foundation of a good diet. Any doubts as to completeness, or particular symptoms, can be rectified by including some of the supplements available, and the foods discussed in this book, which may be particularly rich in a specific nutrient or group of them.

CHAPTER ONE

HONEY

Long before sugar, even in its raw state, was known to man, he used honey as a natural sweetener. He collected it from the nests of wild bees, which inhabited many countries of the world even in ancient times, and then he began to discover that it was a medicine as well as a food. The medical books of the ancients describe the use of honey for coagulating the blood and curing infection when applied to wounds, soothing and healing burns and bruises, curing coughs, colds and sore throats, helping digestion, and in fact acting pretty much as a cure-all. This knowledge they gained by trial and error and today we still use honey in much the same way as people did thousands of years ago, but now we know more about the reasons for its success.

Honey is the best natural sweetener, not only because of the nutriments it contains, but also because it is pre-digested by the bee and therefore the body can put it to instant use as an energy-giver. What this means is that when the nectar is collected by the bee, it contains different types of sugar, including a fair proportion of sucrose, of which white sugar is almost entirely made up. The bees convert the sugars into simple sugars, levulose and dextrose, which can be absorbed straight into the blood stream. Apart from its energy-giving potential, honey is also good for anyone who has problems with digestion because it neutralizes acid.

CONSTITUENTS

Honey is largely made up of sugar, of course, but it also contains valuable elements, of which minerals make up an important part. These are potassium, magnesium, iron, sodium, calcium, phosphorus, sulphur, chlorine, copper, and lime, although the exact proportions vary with the different types of nectar used to produce the honey. The darker honeys contain more minerals than the lighter ones – sometimes four times as much iron, for example.

As well as minerals, honey contains vitamins C, B_2, B_6, K, folic acid, carotene, proteins, and organic acids. When we consider that honey is 17 per cent water and 75 per cent sugar, we can see that these other nutrients do not form a very large part of its make-up. Nevertheless, it is astonishing what they manage to do, presumably because of the precise combination and because the purity of honey gives it anti-bacterial properties. Interestingly, when scientists and nutritionists have tried to break honey down to study its components, and then put it together again, they have been unable to come up with honey. There is a missing ingredient, presumably contributed by the bee, which may be what gives it its particular qualities, or it could be a facet of the pollen in honey.

Once man had begun to realize the importance

of honey in his life, he began to keep bees rather than relying on finding supplies from bees' nests. Today, many people keep colonies of bees in hives, collecting just enough honey not to rob the bees, for obviously they are not going to all that trouble for the sake of their beekeeper owners.

All through the summer months, as soon as the flowers begin to bloom, the worker bees of the colony fly out of the hive to collect nectar and pollen to build up stores for the winter. The colony is made up of one queen, who lays thousands of eggs and is waited on by the other bees; the workers, who look after the queen, forage for supplies, keep the hive clean and tidy, and keep a general eye on the chores round the hive; and the drones who exist solely to fertilize the queen. The bees build up a wax comb in the hive, and the queen lays her eggs in the cells of this. Food supplies are also stored in the cells of the comb. Before the nectar is stored away, though, it goes through various breaking-down processes, whereby it is converted into honey.

REMEDIAL VALUE

Though only present in small quantities, the nutrients in honey are all important to a healthy diet and also to the cure of specific ailments. Vitamin C, of course helps to prevent colds and related ailments, and as the body cannot store it, supplies need to be taken in every day. Because people tend to overcook vegetables (or not eat enough of them in the first place), which are the most usual source of vitamin C, they are often under-supplied and are therefore less resistant to infection, particularly during the winter. Lack of vitamin B_2 can cause eye infections or poor eyesight, nervous problems or skin disorders. It is also needed for the metabolism of fats, proteins and carbohydrates in food. Vitamin B_6 helps in the metabolism of proteins and again lack of it can cause skin problems. Minerals are often lacking in the average diet, and yet are essential to good health. The sugars are energy-givers and honey also acts as a laxative and aids digestion.

Honey is an antiseptic healer for wounds because its ability to absorb moisture enables it to kill bacteria. These antibacterial properties also help in clearing up all sorts of other things, particularly infections of the throat and nose, such as colds and coughs. For colds, take a drink made with honey and cider vinegar in equal amounts added to half a cup of warm water. This soothes raw and inflamed membranes of the throat too. A sore throat can also be eased by a mixture of 1 tablespoonful of honey, 1 tablespoonful of glycerine, $\frac{1}{2}$ tablespoonful of lemon juice, and a little ginger, taken warm; or, simpler still, try a spoonful of honey in a glass of warm milk. A hot toddy is everyone's favourite remedy for the onset of a cold – honey, whisky and lemon juice made into a drink with hot water and drunk as hot as possible has an excellent effect. A straight mixture of honey and fresh lemon juice relieves a bronchial cough, as does clover tea with honey.

IN THE DIET

As a daily tonic and food supplement, honey will be assimilated into the bloodstream more quickly and effectively if it is taken dissolved in a glass of warm water. For this purpose, it should be taken in three daily doses, either a couple of hours before or a couple of hours after a meal – that is, two tablespoonsful dissolved in a glass of warm water at breakfast time, and the same at lunchtime and in the evening. This will be a completely adequate dosage, and indeed it would not be wise to exceed it because the body will have to assimilate too many carbohydrates.

But although honey has a long-standing and widely-known reputation in the treatment of colds and coughs, it has a farther reaching application than this. The list of ailments and conditions which honey has helped is amazingly long. Liver troubles, for example, have benefited from it, as have anaemia, arthritis and rheumatism, ulcers, kidney disorders, eye diseases, heart weaknesses – you name it, someone somewhere has found that honey has helped it. Even Hippocrates, back in the 4th century BC, found that, 'It causes heat, cleanses sores and ulcers, softens hard ulcers of the lips, heals carbuncles and running sores.'

Although honey gives energy, it also acts as a sedative and so is helpful for people who are highly strung or nervy, and for those who have difficulty in sleeping. It should be taken as a three-times-daily tonic for calming nerves, but for the insomniac, honey in a warm drink just before going to bed will help the brain to relax and prepare for sleep.

Honey used externally has already been mentioned in the context of wounds and burns, but a honey mixture can also be applied to chilblains to good effect. A sticky paste is made from honey, flour, glycerine, and egg-white and applied to the chilblains. Although it sounds an unsavoury and somewhat messy mixture, the healing properties of honey once more get to work to relieve and cure painful chilblains quickly. In the case of burns, a salve of honey draws out the heat and pain and prevents the skin from blistering.

With all these things, and particularly if you are planning to take honey as a general tonic and energy-giver, it is important to stick to the routine of taking it. No one is claiming that honey, or any other food supplement, is going to perform overnight miracles, and with one dose, though the sugar content will produce energy quickly, the overall goodness to the system will not be apparent. It needs a period of time, and of course if the rest of your diet consists of poor quality refined foods, honey will not be able to cancel out the effects of these. A balanced diet, as described in the Introduction, is a foregone premise but the food supplements fill up any gaps in the nutrients, both for those who feel all right but want to feel better, and for those who think that they might be able to help a particular problem or disorder.

BEAUTY TREATMENT

As honey nourishes the body, so it also nourishes the skin, and for centuries it has been used in beauty preparations. Cleopatra, they say, bathed in milk and honey.

Dry, tired skin can be given a new bloom and elasticity by applying a face pack made with honey and bran. Or honey can be used on its own, or mixed with a few drops of cider vinegar or lemon juice, which both have astringent properties for an oily skin. None of these unguents is necessarily a pleasure to apply as honey is of course an extremely sticky substance, but it can be removed easily, after leaving for half an hour or so, with warm water. For sagging, tired skin round the eyes, pat on a mixture of egg-white and honey.

The moisturizing content of honey works on dry, chapped skin too, and the vitamins and minerals nourish any type of skin more effectively than synthetic cosmetics because honey is a natural substance with no chemical additions. Remedies and recipes handed down from generation to generation may sound like quaint old folklore in these days of packaged science, but if beauty-conscious women without access to the vast range of creams and lotions we can choose from today, found that honey worked for them, we can learn from their experience.

CHAPTER TWO

CIDER VINEGAR

If your home-made wine has ever gone badly wrong, you will know that the result is like vinegar. And that is exactly how vinegar began its life. In the case of cider-vinegar, it started as apple juice which was invaded by the microbe *acetobacter* during the fermentation process. It seems odd, perhaps, that a product like this can be such a valuable food supplement, but this has been shown to be the case time and time again.

PRODUCING CIDER VINEGAR

Once it was realized that a new health-giving product had resulted from an error in manufacture, cider vinegar began to be made as such. The first stages are the same as for cider, in that the juice is pressed out of the apples and left to ferment so that all the sugar is converted into alcohol. The cider is then left to mature for a few months, after which the *acetobacter* is deliberately introduced in a process called acetification. In the old days, this was done by soaking birch twigs in a mixture of cider and freshly-made vinegar. The bacteria would breed on the twigs and once this had happened the cider was added to the mixture in batches and circulated through the acetifier so that oxygen could reach the *acetobacter*, enabling the alcohol to be converted into acetic acid. This was a slow process, however, during which some of the nutrients of the cider were lost, and acetification is nowadays carried out by an acetifier called 'Fring's Acetator' which converts the cider quickly and under enclosed conditions so that nothing is lost.

NUTRITIONAL COMPOSITION

But what are these vital ingredients that it is so important to preserve? Firstly, cider vinegar contains many of the minerals that are essential to health – potassium, calcium, sodium, phosphorus, copper, and iron. It is also made up of ascorbic acid, vitamin B_2 (riboflavin), nicotinic acid, invert sugars, and acetic acid.

The exact balance of these ingredients varies slightly according to the type of cider vinegar, because each brand is made with a different type of apple, but they all have the effect of acting as an overall tonic for good health as well as being helpful in the treatment of certain ailments.

Cider vinegar has been called a panacea for all ills, always a debatable claim. What it does do, and this is probably the reason for its universal success in the treatment of illnesses, is to supply nutrients that are often missing from the diet, and supply them in such a way that they are absorbed easily into the system, so revitalizing and restoring health and vigour.

As a daily tonic, it should be taken diluted in water – two teaspoonsful to a glass of water –

three times a day. The dilution takes the sharpness out of the taste, giving it quite a pleasant taste. It should be drunk in the morning, at midday and in the evening, so that the doses are well spread out.

But apart from its daily tonic effect, cider vinegar also helps a variety of specific conditions and ailments.

If you are inclined to be overweight, for example, a cider vinegar drink with your meals helps to cut down your appetite for over-stuffing yourself with food because it enables the food to be broken down more efficiently in your body. This does not mean that you can get away with eating starchy and fattening foods and expect cider vinegar to work miracles, but if your diet is well balanced and wholesome, it will help you to slim more effectively. A dilution as described above should be taken first thing in the morning and with every meal.

REMEDIAL VALUE

Ailments for which cider vinegar has worked with many people include asthma, hay fever, arthritis and rheumatism, backache, skin troubles, constipation, digestive conditions, colds, catarrh, sore throats, cataract, cramp, heart conditions, and shingles. From this it can be seen why it has been called a cure-all, for the list is indeed varied. It is often taken combined with honey to make a sweeter tasting drink, or it can be used in cooking, in salad dressings, or whenever vinegar is needed in a recipe.

But why does it work for so many different ailments? To illustrate this point, it may be useful to outline briefly some of the ways in which it can be helpful.

Colds and Sore Throats

If cider vinegar is taken daily as a tonic, it helps to prevent colds developing in the first place by increasing the body's resistance to infection. If you are just starting to take it at the moment you feel a cold coming on, though, you can take it with large doses of vitamin C to either fend off the cold altogether, or at worst make it a milder attack. Sore throats can be soothed by a drink made up of cider vinegar and honey, and the ingredients also help to clear up the infection. It is similarly efficient for coughs and laryngitis, possibly because of its acid content, which kills off the bacteria that cause aggravations of the throat.

Digestion

Research and practical application have shown that potassium and acetic acid balance in cider vinegar aid digestion by eliminating any harmful bacteria in the food and promoting the activities of the essential bacteria which break the food down in the stomach and intestine. The nutrients in the food are therefore absorbed into the body more readily and digestion is smooth. It also aids indigestion and flatulence, or prevents it in those who are normally prone, if the cider vinegar drink is taken with meals.

Constipation or Diarrhoea

The cider vinegar drink can help both these conditions. In the first case, it should be taken three times a day in conjunction with a couple of tablespoonsful of bran. As far as diarrhoea is concerned, provided this is not caused by an infection that needs separate treatment, it too can be alleviated by adding cider vinegar to the extra fluid that is needed to replace that lost with diarrhoea. Water that is usually absorbed by the large intestine is passed straight through the body and this means that you need to take at least two extra pints of liquid a day to replace it, with cider vinegar added as a treatment for the condition itself.

Heart Conditions

The cause of many heart attacks is being overweight and, as has been seen, cider vinegar can help this condition if used in a slimming regime. But this should be done in conjunction with other precautions against heart disease, such as avoiding animal fats like butter, which can cause hardening of the arteries due to the build up of cholesterol, and replacing them with vegetable fats such as corn oil or sunflower seed oil, as well as keeping to a well-balanced diet with plenty of vegetables and very little sugary food. The cider vinegar treatment coupled with general good sense as regards diet also helps sufferers from angina and high blood pressure.

Skin and Hair

Nothing reflects good health so much as the condition of the skin and hair. A taut skin with a healthy colour and shining hair show that all is well within, and people have noticed that after a course of the cider vinegar drink with meals, they not only feel better, but look far brighter too. Maybe this is because cider vinegar provides extra supplements to the diet, maybe it is because it helps digestion and any tendency towards constipation, meaning that impurities in the body are eliminated and the insides are working smoothly in the breaking down of food. This is particularly reflected in the skin, which may become discoloured, blotchy or spotty if all is not well inside. In addition, cider vinegar can be used as an external lotion, though preferably mixed with some perfume as the vinegary smell may not make you very sweet to be with. Again, it is diluted and some people make up a mixture of cider vinegar and an infusion of rosemary which is good for the skin and hair, and can be stored and used gradually. It is a well-known fact that too frequent washing of the hair with most of the shampoos on the market is bad for it because the alkalinity of the shampoo dries out the natural oils in the scalp, making it dry and scurfy. A final rinse with cider vinegar mixed with rosemary and some perfume until the smell is to your liking helps to restore the natural oils to the hair.

From these few examples it can be seen that cider vinegar is a very versatile supplement and therefore also aids general good health, even if you think you are feeling fine. Why not feel even better? But does it matter which sort of cider vinegar you take? Vinegar imported from other countries may contain a different balance of ingredients and therefore not have the same effect, so you should make sure that you know from whence the brand you buy originated, and this should be made clear on the label. The main British brands may vary very slightly, depending upon the type of apple used in manufacture and it may be that you will find one brand to be more efficacious than another for your particular condition.

CHAPTER THREE

YOGURT

Yogurt, these days a popular food to be found in every supermarket in some form or other, was until recently regarded as a very specialized and acquired taste. Even now, some people are not too keen on natural yogurt, unflavoured by fruit, and think it rather odd to eat what is basically sour and curdled milk. Yet, as with cider vinegar, the fermentation process or introduction of bacteria has produced a food that is actually more beneficial to the system than the food from which it originally came. Milk is a food rich in nutrients itself, but some people have a digestion that cannot take it. The lactic acid in yogurt makes it a far more digestible food than milk itself.

Yogurt is known all over the world, but by different names. It can be made from cow's or goat's milk – or for that matter, reindeer's, buffalo's, camel's, ass's, depending on the part of the world you happen to live in. The fermentation process is carried out by introducing lactic acid bacteria, or sometimes yeast, and in doing this, any bacteria in milk that may be unhealthy are destroyed and the organisms that are put in are beneficial ones.

Milk contains a proportion of all the essential nutrients, though it is largely made up of water. It consists of protein, fats and carbohydrates in roughly equal quantities, and a small amount of mineral content. It also has a useful supply of vitamins – B_2, C and D – all important to health.

DIGESTION

For most people, milk is perfectly easy to digest, but those with poor digestion, who are prone to heartburn and other discomforts of this kind may find that it coagulates in the stomach, causing indigestion. Solid food is broken down as we eat it, by chewing and the secretion of saliva which starts the process off – so that hastily gulped-down food normally causes the eater to pay later with pains, or, at best, discomfort.

But with milk, of course, digestion of the 'food' parts – the protein, fats and carbohydrates – cannot begin until the milk has been swallowed and passed into the intestine. So if milk is taken too quickly, or the stomach is not producing sufficient acid to break it down properly, it becomes a solid mass, causing heartburn.

In yogurt, although the food value is much the same as in milk, the casein which causes the coagulated effect during the digestion of milk has been broken down into an easily assimilated state.

Protein can only be digested with the help of acid and the digestive juices produced by the stomach are gastric juices and hydrochloric acid. As people get older, their stomachs may be less efficient in producing hydrochloric acid, and they find difficulty in digesting protein; milk, of course, and other foods such as meat and cheese.

The acid content of yogurt, although it still has the protein content of milk, makes it digestible to those who cannot take the other protein foods, and indeed helps the stomach to digest other proteins. Proteins are an essential constituent of a healthy diet, and so a way round must be found for people who have trouble with them. Yogurt introduced into the diet on a regular basis can provide that way round.

It has been found too that yogurt is helpful for constipation and gastric irritation – in the former case it must be accompanied by a balanced fibre-filled diet including such foods as bran and green vegetables. Doctors have found, though, that patients suffering from gastric irritation have been able to take yogurt when they found it impossible to digest other foods, including milk.

Although everyone is able to digest the lactose (milk sugar) at birth, enabling them to be fed exclusively on milk as babies, some people, due to genetic and environmental factors, lose much of the digestive enzyme, lactase, that is necessary for this. This further problem that can occur in the digestion of milk causes stomach cramps and diarrhoea. This tends to happen more among people who are not brought up to drink milk and milk products after babyhood – the enzyme slowly diminishes until if they later want to take dairy products they find difficulty in doing so, and this can be carried through generations. For example, a race brought up in an area that does not include the keeping of dairy herds and the consumption of dairy products, would experience this difficulty if members of that race moved into a country where drinking milk was the norm – an example seems to be people from some African countries, where milk products are not used much in the adult diet, settling in Britain or America.

Yogurt fermented by lactic acid contains very

little lactose and so again is a food that can be taken as an alternative.

A BRIEF HISTORY

Yogurt and other fermented milk products have been made for centuries all over the world. Many claims for their benefits were made, one of which was that they promoted longevity and sexual prowess, claims not backed up by subsequent studies which show no proof that people living to a ripe old age do so because of yogurt or would not have done so without it. People have made wild claims about most so-called health foods which can denigrate the food itself and make others sceptical about the facts which *are* proven – namely, that combinations of certain nutrients do help both general health and specific ailments.

There are many references to yogurt in ancient writings. Herodotus and Pliny both mention it as being a health-giving food – though under different names from 'yogurt', which originated in Turkey and Bulgaria. Fermented milk is called 'koumiss' in parts of southern Russia and Central Asia, where it is made from mare's milk; 'leben' or 'laban' in the Middle East; 'taette' in Scandinavia; and so on. Kefir originated in the Balkan countries and is yogurt with a small alcoholic content.

In Britain, yogurt as such is a relatively recent arrival, although fermented milk products, in the shape of curds and whey and junket, formed part of the staple diet centuries ago. The curds and whey of Miss Muffet fame were made by separating the solid part of the milk (curds), which also form the basis of cheese, from the water part (whey) by the introduction of acid. Junket used to be made by laying the curds on rushes called 'junci' so that the whey could drain off. It was a food enjoyed on high days and holidays, hence the terms 'junketting' and 'junkets' for holidays, feasts and riotous goings-on.

However, with the dying out of curds and whey (although junket is still regarded as a suitable, if somewhat distasteful, dish for invalids with weak digestion) as a popular food, there was a gap in the use of fermented milk products until yogurt was reintroduced under that name, and nowadays quite a few people, realizing its goodness, make their own yogurt from cow's or goat's milk.

COMMERCIALLY PRODUCED YOGURT

Yogurt should be eaten within a week or so of being made because, although it will keep in the refrigerator for quite a time, the bacterial properties which make it so beneficial begin to dwindle after a week. When buying yogurt in a shop, of course, it is difficult to tell exactly how old it is, although most brands have a selling date on them. However, this does not tell you the date on which the yogurt was made. So bought yogurt may not be particularly beneficial unless it comes from a source where these facts can be discovered.

Another disadvantage of commercially produced yogurt is the ingredients which are added to make it palatable to a wider range of people. Fruit yogurts, for example, have sugar, colouring and preservative added, and some types are made with a mixture of skimmed milk and whole milk, with thickening agents added.

The best way to buy yogurt, if you can, is direct from someone who has a farm or smallholding and makes his own. This way you can find out when it was made, and can also be sure that it is made from whole milk without additives. Alternatively, you can make your own. Once you have set up the equipment, which does not amount to much, you can make it far more cheaply than buying the commercial brands.

HOME PRODUCED YOGURT

You can buy an electrically operated yogurt maker, with which you can pretty well guarantee foolproof yogurt every time. However, the early yogurt makers had no such device, and you do not need one if you prefer to use the more traditional methods.

You will need a good starter to get the fermentation going. To do this, you can buy a fresh starter or, once you have got going, use some yogurt from your previous batch – provided it is new so that the bacteria is still alive. The starter yogurt must be unflavoured. The milk you use must be pasteurized so that there are no alien bacteria to come up against the *lactobacilli* which work on the milk to make it into yogurt. Apart from this criterion, though, the milk can come from cows or goats – and, as has been said, other animals in other countries, such as reindeer in Lapland and camels in the Middle East.

The milk has to be incubated while the fermentation process is taking place – as does wine or beer, though for a longer period – and the time this takes will vary according to the freshness of the milk, the temperature, and the quality of the starter. The milk should be as fresh as possible, to shorten the incubation time.

The milk is brought to the boil and then cooled to blood heat or a little above. At this point the starter is added and the temperature is fairly critical because if it is too cool the bacteria will not multiply efficiently, and if it is too hot they will be killed off.

The culture must be kept at an even temperature during the incubation period, hence the need for an incubator. People have used a variety of devices, from a wide-mouthed thermos to an electric oven at a temperature of between 90°F and 100°F (32°C and 37°C). Vessels for yogurt making should be of stainless steel or enamel, or material that does not affect the process. Once the starter has been added to the milk, it should not be transferred to another container until the incubation is complete. A shorter incubation period at a higher heat (but below 115°F (46°C), at which point the bacteria are killed) makes a mild-tasting yogurt with plenty of good bacteria.

A slower, lower-temperature incubation gives a sharper-tasting yogurt with more lactic acid in it. However, over-incubation should be avoided, and the yogurt should be checked after a certain period to see whether separation is going ahead.

More precise instructions on making yogurt will be found in books about this and other dairy products. But this outline shows that it is easy to produce your own, thus ensuring that you have supplies of this nutritious and beneficial food in peak condition.

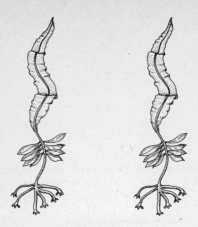

CHAPTER FOUR

KELP

Kelp is another word for seaweed and normally refers to the larger brown or greeny-brown types. In some parts of the world, kelp grows to an enormous size, and in some countries such as Japan, it is specially farmed as a nutritious vegetable and food supplement. There are also kelp crops in Europe, though obviously the countries with the most coastline fare best and the United Kingdom, along with Norway, France, Spain, and Portugal, grow and harvest seaweed.

BENEFICIAL PROPERTIES
Why do this? The thought of eating a plate of seaweed is not a particularly appetizing one when you consider the slimy, tangly plants of seaside holidays. The answer, of course, is that sea plants are far richer in certain nutrients than any land crops. The principal group is minerals, with kelp being at least ten times richer in them than land

plants. It contains phosphorus, potassium, sodium, lead, copper, zinc, and iron, and there is no better source of iodine. Iodine is a mineral that provides the body with physical and mental energy by controlling the metabolism, and at the same time controls obesity by counteracting lethargy and inactivity. Large doses of iodine also cure goitre, which often occurs in communities where the crops are deficient in this mineral. Some other crops do contain iodine, but these tend to be grown in coastal regions, so that it is the environment rather than the plant itself that contributes to the presence of the mineral.

Apart from minerals, kelp is a good source of vitamins, including A, B$_{12}$, C, D, thiamine, niacin, riboflavin, and pantothenic acid, as well as amino acids, trace elements, and a sugar content called manitol which does not increase the blood sugar. Therefore diabetics can take kelp without worrying about this aspect.

Like most natural supplements and remedies, kelp has been known as a beneficial plant for centuries. The Romans used it as fertilizer and food for animals, uses for which it is still known. The Ancient Greeks discovered that it helped intestinal ailments such as diarrhoea, and also goitre, although they did not know why. And it has long been used in Japan where it forms a major part of the diet, as a sea-vegetable and also in the form of extracts and supplements. For example, it can also be used as a thickening agent or solidifier for such dishes as jellies. It can be taken in the form of kelp tablets to give a daily nutritional supplement. It can even be used in the bath, when a soak in a tub containing some extract of seaweed can relieve pain such as rheumatism and even internal ailments like bronchitis.

In the Western world seaweed as a food for people rather than animals is a relatively recent discovery but it has been known about from the Middle Ages when it was used for manures and was also burnt to extract the mineral content, and has been used in farming for many years. Its fortunes have fluctuated as uses for it changed, but today its uses have become established and it is still sold, in liquid form, as fertilizer, and is also fed to livestock. As far as people are concerned, kelp can be added to the diet in a variety of ways, depending upon personal inclination and also on what it is being taken for, and in what quantity. It can be bought in tablets, as has been mentioned, or in powder form to add to cooking; in soap or skin preparations or bath extract for external use, and of course as a sea-vegetable to be eaten as such. Because of its vitamin B_{12} content, which is not contained in many land plants, it is a particularly valuable food for vegetarians, as meat-eaters can get a supply of this vitamin from liver, for example, but those relying on plant foods have more of a problem.

There are various types of packeted kelp which can be bought for cooking with, and a visit to your health food store will help you to see what variety is available in your area. It can come as powder, in dried sheets, bunches or strands, or as sprouts, and these last types are the ones that would be cooked as a vegetable.

CULTIVATION
Seaweed farmers do not merely rely on chance for their supply of kelp, but cultivate special areas with different types and these are cut by hand or by mechanical cutters. When seaweed is grown in beds off the seashore, divers go down and cut the plants, leaving enough of each one for them to grow again, and the cut portions float to the surface where they are collected in a net.

Because some types of seaweed grow very slowly, harvesting has to be done carefully so that

there is a rotating crop and an area is not cut
down too much. This is true of the type grown in
Norway, *ascophyllum*, where seaweed farming is
well established and some of the best crops are
produced. Japan is the forerunner of this kind of
farming, and several varieties are grown around
its coasts and dived for by trained cutters at
harvesting time. The United Kingdom has some
fine seaweed beds too, and in addition dried
seaweeds are imported from such countries as
Japan, giving a variety of types to choose from.

When the seaweed has been cut and collected
in nets, it is taken to factories for drying. This must
be done as soon as possible so that none of the
nutritional value is lost once the plants have been
cut. When it has been dried, the best part of the
crop is set aside for making kelp tablets, powder
and so on, and the rest is used for animal
feedstuffs.

But, apart from in a general sense, how is
seaweed helpful, and for what conditions is it
specially good? Here again, we can look to its
mineral supply for the answer, for it is as a result
of a deficiency in minerals in particular, and
nutritional elements in general, that the disease
and ailments, seaweed helps are caused.

REMEDIAL VALUE

Iodine forms a natural tranquillizer, and is
therefore useful in any condition caused by
nervous tension or neuro-muscular disturbance.
In these painful conditions, too, the symptoms
can themselves cause stress, so that one thing
leads to another, and kelp can prevent some of
this tension with its tranquillizing effects. In
painful nerve or skeletal diseases such as
rheumatism, arthritis, fibrositis, and neuritis, it
acts as a supplier of vitamins and minerals which
the nerves need. These illnesses can of course be
caused by external conditions, such as a poor

climate, but they may also be linked to a nutritional deficiency which not only acts on the joints, nerves and tissues, but stagnates the blood circulation so that impurities are not expelled, and also is biased too much towards acid-forming foods. Kelp is one of the supplements that neutralizes excess acid, because mineral salts are alkaline, cleanses the bloodstream and stimulates the circulation.

Because of these same factors, seaweed acts as a mild and natural laxative, as well as helping intestinal disorders. Constipation is normally brought on by a bad diet, a fact which most people do accept but do not necessarily act upon. Instead they may resort to violent laxatives which act as an irritant rather than a cure. Roughage is needed, of course, in the form of wholewheat bread and cereals, or bran, and fibrous fruit and vegetables. But again, lack of vitamins and minerals often come into the story, and a daily dose of seaweed prevents this. The minerals in seaweed tone up the colon walls and muscles, too, and neutralize excess acid in the diet.

Indigestion or dyspepsia is caused by too much acid-forming food, and so the alkalinity of seaweed, coupled with a more suitable diet, prevents troubles of this sort, and possible ulcers too.

Diarrhoea is caused by the irritation of the mucous membranes in the intestine or bowels, either following constipation or after using a strong laxative, or caused by toxic elements in food. Sometimes it is merely a brief occurrence, when the body is eliminating toxic matter, for example; but if it is prolonged it may be connected with a disease and treatment should be sought. Seaweed, although it acts as a laxative, is also an antiseptic and so soothes the irritated membranes that cause diarrhoea and helps to relieve congestion, such as when the mucous membrane of the intestine is actually swollen and secreting an excessive amount of mucus which has to be eliminated from the body. It also relieves gastric catarrh and mucous colitis, which are caused by irritated mucous membranes.

This ability to soothe and heal irritated mucous membranes acts on other parts of the body too – obviously, anywhere that is lined with mucous membrane and becomes inflamed would react in the same way as the intestines to the antiseptic qualities of seaweed. The mineral salts, as well as purifying and stimulating the bloodstream, help to relieve disorders of the kidneys and bladder (such as cystitis), the liver, gall bladder, pancreas, arteries, and the reproductive organs. The gall bladder, for example, because it is lined with mucous membranes, secretes mucous when irritated, causing a catarrhal condition. Catarrh, caused by irritation of mucous membranes, can generally be avoided by eliminating mucus-forming foods from the diet – too much fatty and fried food and too little alkaline food such as vegetables – and a daily supplement of seaweed helps to neutralize any excess there may still be, thus preventing, in this case, the gall bladder trouble that can lead to gall stones.

It has already been mentioned that seaweed can help bronchitis and here again it is dealing with irritated mucous membranes. Other respiratory ailments therefore come into this category, too – the common cold, laryngitis, influenza, and catarrh. The mucus is more evident, with the habitual blocked-up or runny nose, coughing and sneezing as the body tries to expel the irritation itself. Mucus-forming foods should again be avoided, but this often takes care of itself in any case by the loss of appetite that accompanies most of these ailments. Plenty of liquids such as fruit juice should be taken, and powdered seaweed can be added to these or to soups, to do its work on the mucous membranes and also to step up the vitamin and mineral supply.

Prevention being better than cure, however, a daily dose of seaweed should be taken by anyone with a tendency to catarrh or other respiratory problems. Kelp tablets are probably the easiest way of ensuring an adequate daily quota, but the other methods mentioned earlier can be tried too. Indeed, as its benefits are so wide-ranging and affect so many parts of the body, a daily supplement before any of these problems arise can do nothing but prevent them and give instead a general feeling of health and well-being. Its tranquillizing and cleansing effect can do much to alleviate those slightly below par, tense feelings so many people accept as a matter of course. Although they do not feel exactly ill, neither do they feel exactly well. The accompanying lethargy and tiredness can be replaced by energy and, so the body begins to function more efficiently again. So, as well as being recommended for specific ailments, seaweed acts as a general tonic if taken every day.

CHAPTER FIVE

WHEAT GERM

In days gone by, before the advent of sophisticated milling machinery, people did not even have to think about wheat germ as a separate entity. It was contained in the bread they ate and the flour they baked with. The whole grain, with all its natural roughage and nutrients intact, was there, and bread was wholesome and nutty in flavour. Today, you have to ask for wholewheat bread and make sure that that is what you get before you can get the sort of loaf that will do you good.

A grain of wheat is made up of three main parts. On the outside are layers of bran which form a protective fibrous coating. Beneath this is the endosperm, which is mainly starch, and at the heart of the grain comes the germ, the living part that germinates when the grain is planted.

DENATURED BREAD

Put together, the constituents of wheat grain complement each other, but in the white bread we see today, only the endosperm is used, so that all the nutritious content is lost. The bran layers are husks and the bread needs more chewing if they are left in. The wheat germ, being the living part, causes wholewheat flour to go mouldy after a while, whereas white flour will keep indefinitely. So what we are getting is solid starch made from the dead substance of the grain. People may think they prefer it because it keeps well, has a moist blotting-paper substance that makes it easy to cut, and is generally more convenient. A white sliced loaf requires no effort and has been with us for many years now. We are so used to bread that tastes of nothing that children often think they don't like 'brown bread'. In a sandwich, you can taste the bread as well as the filling and this may seem all wrong to someone who is used to its being merely something to hold the filling in place.

The term 'brown bread' is deceiving too, of course, because as such it means nothing. Indeed, white flour may have colouring added to make it brown, or a loaf may be described as 'wheatmeal' which should not be confused with 'wholewheat' for the whole grain is not used. Any bread but wholewheat will be less satisfying, meaning that people eat more of it and, as they are eating largely starch, they put on weight and add nothing to their good health.

NUTRITIONAL VALUE

So what is wheat germ and why does it matter whether we eat it or not? The answer is that it is an excellent source of vitamins which we have to include in our diets in some other way if we eat bread from which the wheat germ has been extracted.

Bread made from wholewheat is not the only source of wheat germ, of course. You can use wholewheat flour for your baking, eat only wholewheat cereals and buy wheat germ as a separate product to add to food. The germ of the wheat grain is richer in nutrients than that of other cereals such as barley, rye or oats. Wheat has been grown for thousands of years and was first developed by crossing two grasses, dinkel and wild emmer, which grow in mountainous areas, to produce a grass with an edible and nutritious grain, and finally the crop we know today. The result is a germ which contains protein as well as vitamins A, the B complex, and E. Naturally, all these ingredients can be found in other foods, but wheat germ is a concentrated source. Vitamin A is found in green vegetables such as cabbage and lettuce, and in plants it is known as carotene. There are two other categories of vitamin A – A_1 and A_2, the former found in the livers of salt-water fish and the latter in the livers of freshwater fish. Obviously enough, it is carotene that most of us will get in our diets, provided they contain plenty of green vegetables. But vegetables lose nutrients in the cooking so unless you eat them raw or concentrate on such things as watercress and lettuce, they will not be such effective sources of supply. So wheat germ as an alternative or additional food for vitamin A is important, particularly in the winter when raw vegetables and salads may not seem so appetizing and indeed are hard to come by.

VITAMIN A
Vitamin A is needed for healthy skin, good eyesight, growth in children, and protection of the respiratory tract. Night blindness is sometimes a result of a lack of this vitamin because it helps the eyes to react to light and adjust accordingly. It has been found that adults need about 2500 international units of vitamin A each day (there is

no advantage in taking more, and it can be a bad thing to greatly exceed the level of any one dietary constituent). This measurement probably does not mean a great deal, but what it boils down to is that you would have to eat 1000g or 2 lb of bread if you were relying on wheat germ alone. This is of course neither feasible, nor desirable, but it does show that nibbling a lettuce leaf will not do the trick. However, a balanced diet containing plenty of vegetables, wholewheat bread and cereals, perhaps some supplementary wheat germ, and fish liver oil, such as cod or halibut, will provide more than enough for good health.

VITAMIN B

The B complex consists of several different vitamins which have been isolated out and found to be necessary for various aspects of health. Vitamin B_2 (riboflavin) has already been mentioned as being necessary for eyes, nerves and skin, Vitamin B_1 (thiamin) is mainly needed for the muscles and nervous system, particularly the nerves of the eye. A deficiency can cause a breakdown of the nervous system that makes the eye function efficiently. Children also need it for growth. Apart from wheat germ and other whole cereals, the main sources of the B vitamins are yeast and liver – a fairly limited selection, particularly for vegetarians. Vitamin B_6, as we have seen, is needed for the metabolism of proteins and also for general good health. Wheat germ is one of the richest sources of B vitamins which are necessary for health and growth, and particularly for eyesight.

VITAMIN E

Wheat germ is the best source of vitamin E there is, a vitamin mainly connected with fertility and, more recently, the prevention of heart disease. Severe vitamin E deficiency can cause sterility in the male and a tendency to miscarriage in women. In the latter case, if the deficiency is diagnosed and the woman is given a diet with plenty of vitamin E in it, one miscarriage would not be followed by another. There are of course plenty of other reasons for miscarriage, but the vitamin can be used as a precaution against possible miscarriage because it helps the placenta to become established in the wall of the uterus. Vitamin E deficiency causes the placenta to lose its hold on the uterus wall and come away. It has been shown in tests that women who were prone to miscarry could complete a preganancy, when given vitamin E in the form of wheat germ oil. This evidence cannot be called conclusive because many women have had children after repeated miscarriages and, further, in the tests a small percentage of the women still had miscarriages with the vitamin E supplement. However the tests still suggest that a precautionary daily dose of vitamin E may well help the situation, and that an adequate amount should be taken as part of the diet.

In the case of sterility, however, wheat germ does no good at all, as tests on sterile women proved very conclusively. The answer here is that the diet should never be allowed to get so low in vitamin E that this is caused in the first place, since green vegetables, eggs, milk, and seed oils provide it as well as wheat germ.

Vitamin E also tones up muscles, prevents constipation and enriches the blood, so that it is a preventative against anaemia. It has also been found to relieve heart conditions by making the muscles work more efficiently, thus taking strain off the heart. The heart muscles need more oxygen without vitamin E, causing breathlessness and straining the heart, and it has been found in some cases that it can relieve hardening of the arteries.

From this brief summary it can be seen that the tiny germ at the heart of a grain of wheat contains much that we need for our daily health. Those who give us our soft white bread are depriving us of all these nutrients for none is contained in the endosperm. If you eat white bread, you are merely filling yourself up with starch and must get your nutritional supplies from other sources. Surely it is far easier to eat only wholewheat bread and cereals, or if you are not a great bread person, you can take a spoonful or two of wheat germ each day, perhaps sprinkled on cereal, to which it gives a pleasant nutty flavour, and provides only the part of the grain that you want for its proteins and vitamins. You can even sprinkle it on salads or eat it as a cereal with milk and sugar. But in whatever form it is taken it is a valuable food to include in your diet.

CHAPTER SIX

COMFREY

The country name for comfrey is 'boneset' because it has been known for hundreds of years as a plant that has the power to mend broken bones, a supposition that would seldom be believed today. However, as we have seen over and over again, the ancients in discovering their medicines had only trial and error to go by, so that if a thing worked it worked, though they did not really know why. So today, herbalists have come to find, more scientific reasons for the belief that comfrey does indeed possess healing powers for a variety of ills, including that of helping to knit together fractured bones.

THE PLANT
Comfrey is a wild plant which grows in the hedgerows and at the edge of ditches. It is tall with large leaves and bell-shaped flowers, but because of its renewed popularity, people are

beginning to cultivate it in their gardens. It is easy to grow and propagate and can be eaten in the same way as spinach. The leaves can also be made into comfrey tea, or into poultices, lotions and ointments for the treatment of external ailments such as bruises and wounds.

Comfrey is sometimes thought of as the forgotten herb because, although considered to be a cure-all and wonder remedy by the herbalists in days gone by, it is now hardly known of. As with many of these old remedies, the ills they used to cure are now treated with drugs and many people would not know comfrey if they saw it growing in the countryside. Yet, apart from its specific uses, it is one of the most nutritious vegetables that one can find. As far as written records can tell us, the plant has been known all over the world for nearly 2,000 years – and there are about twenty-five species of it which are native to Asia, Europe and Russia.

Russian Comfrey was first brought to England in the nineteenth century, and has now become a cultivated plant of this country. It is taller than common comfrey and has pink and blue flowers. Some varieties have purple, red, white, or yellow flowers, and leaves with white or gold margins.

HEALING POWERS

Like seaweed, comfrey contains vitamin B_{12} and, as has been mentioned, there are very few land plants which can extract this vital nutrient from the soil. But comfrey's most interesting ingredient is probably allantoin, from whence comes its power to help wounds heal. Allantoin is contained in plants generally, but in such minute quantities as to be barely noticeable. Comfrey is the only plant so far discovered which supplies an appreciable amount and the juice of the plant has been used to cure fractures, scarred tissue, wounds, and ulcers. Different types of comfrey contain varying amounts of allantoin and it has been found that where it is present in the largest quantities, the healing power for these ailments is more positive, singling it out as the probable secret of this remedy. Research into uses of allantoin shows that it stimulates tissue granulation, and it is included in ointments and lotions for healing and anti-irritant uses, particularly in the case of infected wounds (or those that are slow to heal) and skin conditions such as dryness and chapping.

SOURCE OF VITAMINS A, B and C

Vitamin B_{12} has to be extracted from the soil and few plants can perform this feat. Comfrey has long roots which can penetrate deep into the subsoil and so draw the vitamin out. Indeed, alfalfa, which has even longer roots, is the only other land plant that we know of as being able to do this, and alfalfa is of course harder to come by in this country, being a native of America. Products including comfrey or alfalfa can be bought at health food shops, but in the case of comfrey, a crop growing in the garden can provide an ever-ready vegetable that contains two important and rarely found nutrients.

Comfrey contains the other B vitamins, as well as vitamins A and C, and a good range of minerals, including iron, manganese, phosphorus, and calcium.

So with all this going for it, comfrey is obviously nutritious. But it is also mucilaginous. This means that it has a soothing effect, not only illustrated by its uses as an anti-irritant and wound healer, but also by its effectiveness against colds, sore throats and other respiratory infections. It will soothe and help to heal internal as well as external ulcers, sprains, muscular strains, and skin conditions such as boils, bruises and even sunburn.

COMPOST AND FEEDSTUFF

Comfrey, if it is known at all, is often more widely recognized for its use as a compost plant and feedstuff for animals. The organic gardener would find it a useful addition to a compost heap because of its mineral and vegetable protein content, enabling it to break down other vegetation efficiently. Although this may not seem a particularly relevant comment to those who are considering buying some comfrey tablets or ointment, or trying a helping or two as a vegetable, it is included to show that its uses as a garden crop are twofold. As a farming or smallholding crop it is equally healthy food for cattle, horses and pigs.

COMFREY AS A CROP

If you plan to grow comfrey, it is as well to remember that it does not grow well from seed – or, at least, it takes so long that it is far better to get hold of cuttings to start your crop from. Then it is an easy plant to grow. The bed should be thoroughly weeded before the cuttings are planted, and always kept free of weeds and grass as these will choke the plants.

Plant the cuttings 60cm apart, with the same distance between rows. Comfrey has very long roots, so the soil should be well dug beforehand. The plants should be watered and given an initial feed of compost or manure to get them going. After this they get their nutrition from the soil and only need a sprinkling of poultry manure in the spring and lime in the autumn.

Crops can be planted at any time of year, except in the middle of winter. Spring plantings can be cut in July, but if you have planted in the summer or later, the plants should not be cut until the following year so that they build up strength and become established. Once they have been cut for the first time, you can cut the leaves off about once a month, using the tender ones for vegetables, comfrey tea and so on, and the tougher ones on the compost heap or used for animal feeds. So once established, comfrey is a prolific plant that will provide a good source of vegetables from a few plants (say, six to start with). You can easily increase your crop, too, by cutting the plant right down to soil level and splitting it in two with a spade. You can then slice each section and plant all those that have a growing tip separately to form a new plant. You can produce about fifteen new plants from one stem, and the remains will grow as well.

THE COMFREY SCARE

Despite the fact that comfrey has been taken internally in one form or another for hundreds of years, a scare began recently in which people were warned that it had dangerous properties that could cause cancer of the liver. This has since been considered an alarmist exaggeration of the situation and, though comfrey was taken off the health food shops' shelves for a while, during which time tests were carried out, qualms about its use have largely been eased by the resulting evidence.

The research began in Australia where scientists discovered that comfrey, in common with other plants such as borage and heliotrope, contained an alkaloid which if taken in sufficient quantity can cause liver damage leading to cancer. Tests were carried out by giving this alkaloid to small animals in very high dosages, and in some cases toxic effects were detected. As a result, comfrey users became alarmed and stopped using the herb until further findings had been published.

COMFREY RESEARCH

Probably the leading authority on the cultivation and use of comfrey is the Henry Doubleday

Research Association, where comfrey has been propagated and studied for many years.

Henry Doubleday was a Quaker smallholder from Essex who first brought Russian comfrey (*Symphytum asperum*) back to England from St Petersburg in 1870. He spent the last thirty years of his life studying its cultivation and healing properties. The Association, named in his honour and now the world's largest association of organic gardeners, was founded some 25 years ago by Lawrence D. Hills to carry on this work and other studies into the growth and benefits of plants. Much of the research at 'garden level' is carried out by the Association's members all over the world, and also on the Association's trial ground in Essex. Here too are laboratories where specialist tests and experiments can be carried out, and it is from this source that much if not all of the evidence of the benefits of comfrey have emerged over the years.

Now, in the face of the comfrey scare, the Association have conducted their own tests into the use of this plant and in July 1978 issued a warning to comfrey users to stop taking it until further evidence had been produced. This, it was emphasized, was merely to be on the safe side because the risks were extremely small. The Association had received a letter from a scientist in Australia who believed that comfrey should not be taken internally until further investigations had been carried out.

The Henry Doubleday Research Association in Australia amassed accounts of the successful use of comfrey over long periods, both for feeding livestock and as a medicine for humans. They also sent a questionnaire to their members to find out how many had used comfrey as a vegetable for long periods, and with what results. Vegans are the most likely to take it in large quantities to replace the vitamin B_{12} they are missing in animal foods. They also arranged blood tests for comfrey users which should show up any malfunction of the liver.

In the UK, the Association arranged with Exeter University (where the comfrey alkaloids have been studied by experts in the field) to carry out tests on comfrey products. Comfrey ointment was shown to contain only three parts per million of alkaloid, and so, as with fresh or pulped leaves used as dressings or poultices, was judged entirely safe. Unlike a substance like DDT, which builds up to dangerous levels in body fats, the alkaloids in comfrey cannot be absorbed through the skin. However, it is thought that the alkaloids in those comfrey products taken internally (for example, in tablet form or tea made with fresh or dried leaves) can have a cumulative effect over a long period.

RECENT EVIDENCE AND CONCLUSIONS

Yet there is evidence provided by a race-horse owner who had fed comfrey to his horses for forty years. Post mortems are carried out when expensive horses such as these die, and in no case was there any sign of liver damage.

But there the findings rested until further and more detailed tests had been completed, and the next report, which seemed to have no doubts as to continued safe use of comfrey, came from the Scientific Committee of the British Herbal Medicine Association. They pointed out in a subsequent statement that no toxicity has been found in human beings, despite the fact that comfrey has been used as a food and a medicine for centuries, and the National Institute of Medical Herbalists have found no such indications in the studies of people taking regular dosages.

Apart from anything else, as far as the United Kingdom is concerned, the statement goes on to point out that the species of comfrey found in Australia, where the first tests were made, is different from that found here, namely *Symphytum officinale L.* Despite this fact, of course, any plant coming under the blanket name of comfrey was up for scrutiny, and tests on rats carried out in conjunction with the British Medical Research Council showed none of the symptoms produced in the Australian tests, and no sign of liver damage was detected.

Dried comfrey, from which comfrey products are made, the statement continues, in any case contain an enzyme that destroys any trace of the suspect alkaloid during the drying process. But even if this were not the case, using the Australian evidence as a yardstick for calculation and transferring these statistics from small animals to man, 'a $12\frac{1}{2}$ stone man would need to drink four large, long-brewed, concentrated cupsful of comfrey tea every day for 100 years to be exposed to even a possibility of any reaction'.

It is worth remembering, too, if the word alkaloid seems to be an alarming one where comfrey is concerned, that potatoes contain the same alkaloid as deadly nightshade!

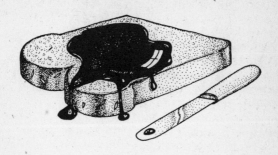

CHAPTER SEVEN

MOLASSES

The white sugar controversy is becoming old hat nowadays, but people nevertheless continue to eat it, just as they continue to eat white bread. Molasses is one ingredient of the sugar cane that is discarded during the sugar refining process, yet it is the part that contains the most goodness.

DENATURED SUGAR
The sugar cane growing on the plantation contains vitamins and minerals, and of course too much fibre for the human system to cope with. Once the sugar had been discovered, more than 2,000 years ago, some form of extraction process was devised and the cane was spread more widely and planted all over the world. Until fairly recently, the sugar was extracted impurities and all, and emerged in a dark brown form which was considered unattractive. In order to get the pure white sugar we know today, everything was

removed from the raw sugar except the sucrose, which has no nutritive value at all. The raw brown sugar which can be bought contains molasses and hence the vitamins and minerals provided by the original cane.

REMOVING THE MOLASSES

When the cane is cut, it is taken to a mill for crushing, at which point the cane juice is squeezed out. The juice is then filtered to remove impurities and passed into a heating vessel to coagulate. Once the solid part has been separated from the juice, the juice passes into evaporators to begin a concentration process. When it begins to crystallize it is separated once again, by centrifugal force, to produce two separate products, molasses and raw sugar. At this point the molasses go through the process again so that more sugar is extracted, but the less boiling and extraction that happens, the more molasses remains in the sugar. The raw sugar is then refined by further filtering and decolourizing until it is really nothing but sucrose.

Molasses, therefore, though discarded, contains everything else and is a concentrated food supplement rich in vitamins and minerals. It may not be to everyone's taste, as it is dark and treacly, but it can be added to cooking in place of sugar, or used in various ways other than taking it by the spoonful.

NUTRITIONAL CONTENT

An analysis of molasses shows that it contains minerals, including iron, calcium, potassium, sodium, magnesium, sulphur, chlorine, and phosphate; the vitamins biotin, niacin, pantothenic acid, and riboflavin in appreciable quantities and other vitamins in lesser quantities; several amino acids and sugars, and protein. It may seem that all the food supplements talked about contain a list of nutrients so that there is not much to choose between one and the other, and indeed they all do. But it is the balance and ratio of these ingredients that make the various supplements act in their different ways, making some more suitable for some things and others for other things, but making them all equally valuable as health-giving foods.

VITAMINS

In the case of molasses, its high vitamin and mineral content act together to make it, for one thing, a useful laxative, despite its lack of roughage. Lack of vitamin B_1 is a common cause of constipation as well as lack of fibrous food, and molasses contains a goodly amount, as do wheat germ, bran, yeast, kelp, green vegetables, and dairy produce. However, the combination of this vitamin with the minerals potassium and calcium, help the muscular movement of the intestine, making molasses a good natural laxative.

MINERALS

Three particularly important minerals contained in molasses, to a greater or slightly lesser extent depending upon the quality of the product, are iron, calcium and potassium.

IRON

Iron, as we know, is vital for the red blood corpuscles and iron tonics are prescribed in cases of anaemia. Far better to take a spoonful of molasses daily, for the iron is assimilated into the body from molasses even more readily than that contained in high-iron-content meat like liver or steak. About 20mg per day of iron is required by an adult. It is stored in the liver, spleen and kidneys, after a small amount has been absorbed into the small intestine. It is circulated round the

bloodstream, muscles and tissues to provide the
essential haemoglobin in the red blood
corpuscles. A tablespoonful of molasses, or the
equivalent included in cooking or put with other
foods, should be a daily supplement for everyone,
but those who suffer from anaemia, poor blood
circulation or heavy menstruation should take 2
tablespoonsful a day and include molasses
whenever possible in their diet. For example, it
can be used instead of sugar on cereals or muesli,
or in baking and sweet dishes, and even in spicy
and savoury dishes where a touch of sweetness is
needed, perhaps to offset a sharp taste. If you
want to use molasses but can't stand the taste –
though, as has been said, this is only a rather
heavy, treacly one – you can dilute your daily
molasses supplement in a glass of warm water, or
water and milk, and drink it.

CALCIUM

Calcium is needed for strong bones and teeth and
so is particularly important for growing children.
It must be balanced by sodium, which happens
naturally in molasses. Calcium is also necessary,
with potassium and sodium, for muscle tone, and
helps the clotting of the blood. Calcium
deficiency can often be detected by brittle or
speckled nails.

POTASSIUM

Potassium is mainly present in the cells of the
body and, in relation to calcium, is closely related
to muscle tone and function as has already been
mentioned. This is one of the minerals that makes
molasses an effective laxative, because potassium
prevents nervous irritability, again balanced with
calcium. It also helps the kidneys to function
effectively, and with iron is a blood-building
mineral that should be taken by women suffering
from heavy menstruation.

AMINO ACIDS

Apart from minerals and vitamins, molasses contains about half of the amino acids that are needed by the body to maintain the cells and tissues. Amino acids are normally contained in the protein foods – dairy produce, meat, fish and nuts, and everyone should be eating these foods in goodly quantities anyway, so keeping up their protein supply. Molasses, however, provides a useful extra source that, unlike the protein foods, is alkaline rather than acid.

WHITE SUGAR – ITS DANGERS

So it can be seen, in part at least, what molasses has that white sugar has not. All the ingredients that have been talked about here have been extracted from the white sugar – and this does mean *all*. White sugar does in fact do harm as well as doing no good. Because the sucrose comes in such a concentrated form, unbalanced by any other nutrients, it causes problems with teeth, for example, and weight and skin disorders. So, while it has a sweetening effect, it cannot bolster this up with any goodness. The natural sugars – honey, molasses, treacle, and dark brown sugar (provided it is genuine raw sugar and not doctored up to look brown!) – can satisfy a sweet tooth just as effectively but does you a lot more good.

In the early days, long before refining processes had been introduced, sugar of course contained most of the molasses from the cane, and was used as a medicine as well as a food. By about 600 AD the cane had been taken by the Arabs from Persia to the Mediterranean, and as early as this it was known for its effects on the intestines and the bloodstream. Again, we can only go on theories that have been handed down through the years, but the fact that they have been passed on and stand up to analysis today speaks well for them since man had nothing but guesswork to rely on.

BLACKSTRAP MOLASSES

The term 'blackstrap' molasses is an American one used to refer to molasses from sugar cane, derived in the process of sugar manufacture, and this name should be looked for on any that is bought, for it is on blackstrap molasses that the analyses of nutrients have been made. The exact proportion of ingredients will vary slightly with different types of blackstrap molasses, but in general terms the vitamin and mineral content will always be high.

Nowadays, molasses has become acceptable as a food supplement and indeed, since the increased awareness of dietary needs and today's refined foods has begun, more and more people are setting aside white sugar for one of its natural counterparts. Once you have done so, too, it is very difficult to once again accept that extra sweet and sickly taste of the white product. Like the difference between the tasteless white bread and the nutty wholemeal, white sugar emerges as a very poor relation that has somehow been slipped to us as a way of life without our realizing there was an alternative. Two of the alternatives have been talked about in this book, and with them alone there is no need ever to touch a granule of white sugar again and still get the energy-giving boost of sugar, together with the tonic effects of balanced and natural nutrients thrown in.

CHAPTER EIGHT

SOYABEANS

Not so long ago, soyabeans were thought, if anyone thought about them at all, to be the cranky food of vegetarians, a tasteless and peculiar product if ever there was one. Now, of course, the soyabean needs no introduction really for it has come into its own as a 'vegetable protein', and even for regular meat-eaters has become an acceptable substitute for meat. Apart from health reasons, the soyabean was used as a meat substitute when the price of meat rocketed and it became a luxury for high days and holidays. People – cooks and manufacturers alike – began to experiment with flavours and consistencies and a very tasty product began to emerge, which has now become acceptable to most people in the form of TVP or textured vegetable protein, sometimes specified as soya protein.

CULTIVATION – A BRIEF HISTORY

The soyabean grows best in warm climates, and so is not cultivated successfully in Europe. However, the USA exports a large amount and it is also grown in Asia where it has long been an important crop. It was first cultivated in China where it was held in such high esteem that it was known as 'the meat of the soil' – and records of its first cultivation in China go back four or five thousand years. Here and in Japan it was thought to be one of the five sacred grains, because of its nutritional value, along with rice, wheat, barley, and millet.

From its beginnings in the Far East, the soyabean was probably taken to the USA from Japan during the nineteenth century, but its nutritional value to humans was not realized at first, and it was mainly used for feeding animals and as fertilizer. Later in the century however, its potential began to be seen, and more varieties were brought into the country from Asia. By the early twentieth century, America had become one of the world's largest growers of soya, and it is from there that much of the world supply comes today.

A PROTEIN SOURCE

Soya is a prime provider of protein for vegetarians and vegans, as 40 per cent of the bean is made up of protein. In addition to its protein content in general terms, it has the advantage of containing a distribution of all twenty-two amino acids that make up protein.

The oil in soya is of course vegetable oil, which is less fattening and more healthy than the animal fat found in meat. Soya is also rich in lecithin, the advantages of which are discussed in a later chapter.

Like many of the other foods talked about in this book, soya also contains good amounts of vitamins and minerals, particularly vitamins A, B, C, and E, and the minerals iron, copper, zinc, manganese, calcium, magnesium, nitrogen, phosphorus, potassium, and sulphur.

The advantages of these nutrients have been talked about in other contexts, but they all add to the overall quality of soya. But it is its protein content that is most important because the body is made up of protein in the form of cells, which make up the tissues.

PROTEIN IN THE DIET – THE RIGHT AMOUNT

The body can only store a small amount of protein, yet it needs an adequate daily intake to build up the cells and keep them in good health. A deficiency of protein leads to cell deterioration, lack of energy, and eventually loss of muscle strength and tone. A variety of ills can result from protein lack, but in general terms the body will lose its strength and resistance, circulation will be poor and the bloodstream sluggish. A person who is relaxed needs less protein than one who is living a stress-filled life, rushing and commuting and worrying. Anxious and worrying types will burn up more protein than those who sit back and let things roll. By a similar token, people with a weight problem have to keep an eye on their protein intake or they may have too *much* calorie-wise, but people who are thin and burn up a lot of energy will need more than average. As with most foods, there is no advantage, and possibly some disadvantage, in taking too much and a great disadvantage in taking too little. The *right* amount for every individual must be sought, and integrated into a fully balanced diet.

Soya these days can be bought in many forms, though it starts life as a row of beans in a pod. The bean can be sprouted to give shoots that are very rich in vitamin C. These have long been used in Chinese cookery, both as a vegetable ingredient for dishes or as a salad. Another well-known derivative of the bean that comes from Chinese cuisine is soya or soy sauce, though people may not have realized as they sprinkled it on a plate of Chow Mein, that they were getting nutritional value as well as flavour.

MEAT SUBSTITUTE

I have already mentioned the uses of soya as a meat substitute, and the fact that this is becoming quite a popular food, even for meat eaters who are health or money conscious. It is made up into a variety of different flavours, so that you can buy mock lamb, beef, chicken or whatever, and often herbs and spices are added to make very tasty hamburger and rissole mix. There is no need nowadays for the vegetarian to make do with the distinctive taste of peanuts only, for the health food manufacturers continue to bring out new recipes in pre-packed form. And for those who want to substitute soya meat into their own recipes, it can be used in the same way as real meat, or for non-vegetarians, some real meat and some soya can be mixed to cut down on cost and animal protein.

Textured protein, or soya meat substitutes, normally come in dehydrated form, which has to be soaked in water before use, or canned which can of course be used straight away, and so are handy to keep in the store cupboard for impromptu cooking as well.

SOME OTHER USES

The soyabean is also used to produce soya milk and milk products such as cream and ice cream. There is also soya flour, which can be used for making bread and cakes. Soya bean oil is probably already familiar as a vegetable cooking or salad oil.

So the range of products, and hence ways in

which soya can be eaten every day, is large and new ways of using it are always being tried out. As more and more people begin to worry about the effects of cholesterol on the arteries and overweight caused by eating fatty foods (both of which contribute in a big way to heart disease and failure), they are coming round to the view that animal protein, far from being a strictly necessary part of the diet, should only be taken in moderation, as should all foods made with animal fats, such as butter, cheese and lard. For all these foods vegetable substitutes can be found which reduce the cholesterol intake and contain easily assimilated fats. They also have other nutritional ingredients which add to a healthy diet, besides the very essential protein. One of the products that is making this substitution possible in such an effective way is the soyabean.

Some Ideas for Using Soya
Once you have bought your packet of meat substitute, what do you do with it? You can use it in recipes where meat is normally included, and a few recipes are given here to show how it can be substituted, and in what a variety of ways.

Goulash
4 oz. (100g) beef soya chunks
seasoned flour
2 tablespoonsful oil
2 onions, chopped
1 green pepper, seeded and chopped
3 tablespoonsful tomato paste
14 oz. (400g) can of tomatoes
1 clove garlic, crushed
bouquet garni or pinch of mixed herbs
2 level teaspoonsful paprika
salt and pepper

Add the soya chunks to a pan of boiling water and simmer for 20-30 minutes. Drain and when cool, toss in the seasoned flour and paprika. Fry the vegetables and garlic in the oil until tender and add the soya. Cook for 5 minutes. Add the tomatoes and tomato paste and simmer until heated through and tender. Season.

Moussaka
4 oz. (100g) soya beef mince
1 large aubergine
1 large onion, chopped
2 cloves garlic, crushed
$\frac{1}{4}$ pint (150ml) vegetable stock
2 tablespoonsful tomato paste
salt and cayenne pepper
6 oz. (175g) grated cheese
2 tablespoonsful oil
bayleaf

Simmer soya mince for 2 minutes to hydrate (or see intructions on packet). Fry onions and garlic until tender, and remove from the pan. Fry the sliced aubergine until brown, then sprinkle with salt and drain on kitchen paper to remove any bitter taste. Meanwhile simmer the mince, stock, tomato paste, and bayleaf for about 10 minutes. Place in an ovenproof dish in alternate layers of mince, onion, aubergine, and grated cheese, finishing with the cheese. Bake for 50 minutes at 350°F (177°C or Gas Mark 4), until top is browned.

Curry
4 oz. (100g) soya beef chunks
1 onion, chopped
2 tablespoonsful curry powder
1 teaspoonful cummin
1 teaspoonful coriander
vegetable oil
$\frac{1}{2}$ teaspoonful crushed chillies, or chilli powder
1 clove garlic, crushed

Hydrate the soya by simmering in boiling water for 20 minutes. Sauté the onion in the oil for 10

minutes, until soft but not brown. Add the soya
chunks, curry powder and spices, and garlic, and
simmer, adding extra liquid if necessary, for 20
minutes in a covered pan. Serve with brown rice.

Stew
4 oz. (100g) beef soya chunks
2 onions, sliced
$\frac{1}{2}$ lb (225g) carrots, sliced
8 oz. (225g) tin tomatoes
2 oz. (50g) mushrooms, sliced
Marmite
Bayleaf
1$\frac{1}{2}$ pints (825ml) vegetable stock
salt and pepper

Hydrate the soya beef in the stock and add the
vegetables and other ingredients. Simmer for
about 30 minutes, or until all the vegetables are
tender. Thicken with a little flour if necessary.

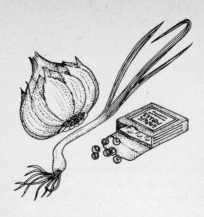

CHAPTER NINE

GARLIC

Known chiefly for its culinary uses and the resultant somewhat anti-social smell, garlic, has for centuries been a medicinal herb as well as a food. Its uses in this context are in fact a direct result of the oil which gives garlic its very strong and distinctive smell, and acts as an antiseptic against germs and infection.

Garlic is a member of the Lily family and, as most people will know, comes in bulbs containing several cloves. It is a cheap herb to buy, for a clove of garlic goes a long way in a dish, so that a bulb lasts a long time. It has been adopted more in this country with the introduction of foreign recipes and restaurants (for it is a vital ingredient of the kitchen in, say, France or Italy) but does not usually appear in English dishes. Nevertheless, the taste if not the odour it leaves behind, has become very popular and as such the herb needs no introduction.

Because it needs plenty of sun over a long period, and is anyway quite cheap to buy, people often do not bother to include garlic in a herb garden, though it is quite possible to grow it in this country. Most of our garlic supplies are imported from the Mediterranean countries, where it grows in abundance. Wild garlic grows in the hedgerows, and even though it is not the same as the garlic we know, and is in fact a member of the mustard family, it still has the strong garlicky smell even when growing, and used to be a favourite garden herb in days gone by.

EARLY MEDICINAL APPLICATIONS

The Babylonians
Once again using the evidence of the Ancients as a starting point for singling out beneficial foods and medicines from natural sources, we can trace the uses of garlic back to 3000 years BC to Babylon, where it was taken for plagues and epidemics, respiratory infections and skin complaints, among other things.

The Greeks
In Ancient Greece, too, the medicinal applications of garlic appear in writings by Aristotle, who talks of it as a tonic and laxative, and Hippocrates, who also names it as a laxative as well as a diuretic. Both these men lived about 400 years BC and were eminent names of their time, who studied deeply the evidence around them. It is interesting, therefore, that garlic should have been singled out for their comments.

The Romans
Galen, a Roman physician of nearly 2000 years ago, praised garlic as an antidote against poison, and Dioscorides, who was physician to the Roman army at around the same time, also used garlic

extensively as a cure for stomach and intestinal complaints and respiratory infections. Another Roman whose writings have been handed down to us, Celsus, also talks about garlic in his Encyclopaedia, where he calls it a cure for many illnesses, and again mentions intestinal disorders.

The Egyptians
But it was in Ancient Egypt that garlic was really well thought of and documented. Even today, members of the onion family – onions, leeks, shallots and garlic – are heavily cultivated in Egypt, and garlic has been known to be eaten there since the building of the pyramids. An inscription on the Cheops pyramid states that garlic was consumed in large quantities by the builders!

A vital part of the Egyptians' medicine chest, too, garlic was taken specifically for skin diseases, respiratory illness, and intestinal disorders, though it was considered a cure-all and miracle herb by them.

A bit nearer to home and more recent was the apparent immunity to the Plague of people who were in contact with garlic at the time. This may sound coincidental, and only supposition supports it, but during the plague in Marseilles in the eighteenth century and the Great Plague in England in 1665, whole families or groups survived without ever contracting the disease, seemingly because large amounts of garlic were stored in their houses. Convicts made to bury the corpses of plague victims in Marseilles also escaped without infection. This was attributed to the fact that they drank wine with garlic (a concoction still known as Four Thieves Vinegar whether the story is apocryphal or not).

GARLIC OIL – ITS ANTISEPTIC PROPERTIES
Although garlic is solidly nutritious, containing a goodly amount of vitamins and minerals, the fact

that only a tiny amount can be eaten with any one meal, for fear of being overpowered by it, these are not really its important factors. As a matter of interest, the bulb is made up of vitamins B and C, some protein, and the minerals potassium, phosphorus and calcium. But the main thing about garlic is its germ-killing potential, which is contained in the oil that produces its strong smell. Unfortunately, because it is this that is so vital, the smell goes with it, and there is no way of avoiding that if you eat garlic by the clove. The only alternative is to take it in the form of capsules or as a product known as Garlic Pearles, which is the oil of garlic in deodorized form. However, the flavour is so good in cooking that it seems a shame to be too inhibited by the smell on the breath, particularly when so many people use it in the kitchen now.

Garlic oil has much the same effect as penicillin, though it acts more slowly because it is not as strong. However, many people notice side effects from penicillin, and there are never side effects from natural remedies, garlic being no exception. When garlic is being taken in largish quantities, to cure rather than prevent perhaps, the use of capsules might come into its own as there is a limit to how much raw garlic it is pleasant to eat! However, with these choices there is no reason not to take garlic as a medicine as well as a flavourer. But what precisely will it do?

MEDICINAL VALUE
On a day-to-day level, it is helpful for such things as colds, coughs and catarrh, as well as more severe bronchial ailments. Take two or three garlic capsules or 1 fluid ounce (25ml) of juice every day, and its expectorant and antiseptic powers will act on the mucous membranes as well as curing the source of infection.

This same antiseptic works on the blood stream,

keeping it pure and free from toxins which can be the cause of all sorts of illnesses. As a blood purifier, it should be taken every day, to prevent things cropping up rather than curing them once they have. Again, capsules are valuable as a supplement if you cannot stomach so much garlic with your food. Skin complaints, for which garlic is also a useful remedy, often arise because of blood impurities, so they should not really occur if it is taken as a daily supplement.

As the Ancients found and reported, garlic also helps intestinal and stomach disorders, acting as a laxative. However some doctors have also found that it cures diarrhoea too.

WILD GARLIC

Should you choose to seek out your garlic in the countryside, as well as buying the more conventional bulbs in a greengrocer, you will find that Wild Garlic, or 'Stinkweed' as it used to be called, can be used in cooking and salads in much the same way, although in this case it is the leaves that are chopped up, when they are young and tender, to add to salads as a dressing or garnish, or to put into casseroles, roasts, soups and sauces, and in fact any dish where you like the flavour of garlic.

Wild Garlic looks rather like lily-of-the-valley when growing, though the latter is poisonous to eat. But there is no danger of confusion for crushing or stepping on the leaves of Wild Garlic will release a pungency that will leave you in no doubt as to what it is. Its medicinal uses are much the same as garlic, too – digestive disorders, blood purification and respiratory ailments.

So garlic, like most of the other supplements, should be taken every day as a prevention of illness and an aid to good health – this will be a better way than waiting till you have a cold or whatever, though it will help them too. But a healthy diet, with the additions mentioned in this book, should go a long way to seeing that you don't suffer in the first place.

CHAPTER TEN

POLLEN

Pollen, the basis of honey and indeed of the bee
itself, comes in minute grains, each of which
contains a miraculous mixture of vitamins,
minerals, amino acids, proteins, hormones, fats,
and enzymes. It is of course the male seed of
plants and flowers, and fertilizes plants which can
then produce new seeds. It can be distributed by
the wind or other natural methods, or it can be
distributed by insects collecting nectar, such as the
bee.

THE BEE AND THE VITAL ROLE OF POLLEN
The bee collects pollen at the same time as nectar.
As it takes the nectar from a flower, grains of the
pollen collect on its legs, so that it can carry back a
double load to the hive, and of course help to
distribute pollen among plants. They visit about
1500 flowers in order to collect enough nectar for

one journey, and consequently pick up a variety of different pollens. It can carry its own weight back to the hive in pollen and nectar.

Back at the hive, the pollen is stored in the cells of the comb until it ferments into 'bee bread'. This is used to feed the larvae, and also to make royal jelly, on which the queen bee feeds. The bee adds saliva and nectar to the pollen grains during its journey, so that the grains can be rolled into a ball and carried back between its knees once the honey sac has been filled.

Pollen is not only collected in passing; it is essential to the lifestyle of the bee. The larvae that feed on it need its ingredients to form their bodies into the amazingly efficient machines they are. Once they begin to develop into bees, all except the queen start eating honey instead of bee bread, but the queen always eats pollen in the form of royal jelly. The inmates of the beehive could not therefore survive without it.

POLLEN HARVESTING

The harvesting of pollen from the hive began in Sweden, where a beekeeper called Costa Carlsson invented a device for collecting some of it as the bees entered the hive on a return flight. The Pollen Food Harvester, as it was called, was a grid put across the entrance of the hive. As the bees passed through the mesh, some of the pollen was brushed off their legs into a container, this is plain pollen, of course, before it has been converted into bee bread or royal jelly, but because these two foods are so vital to the hive, it is important that beekeepers only collect a proportion of the pollen which the bees collect, so that he does not deprive them of their nutrition. Until harvesting of appreciable amounts of pollen could be begun, investigations into its ingredients had been sparse because it could never be collected in large enough amounts, though the value of all the bee products of the hive were appreciated.

POLLEN RESEARCH
After this invention, however, analysis could begin in Sweden to see why it was such a vital food to the bee, and what it contained. The problem was how to break down the minute grains, and once supplies were coming in, research laboratories were set up in Sweden to study pollen. Every plant, flower and tree has a different type of pollen, each one minutely varied, though all containing valuable ingredients. For example, the mineral content of pollen will vary depending upon the type of soil the plant has grown in, so the pollen labs have to isolate pollen grains from soil, and can then microscopically study the individual grains as to size, shape and so on to identify which plant it comes from, and therefore what it contains.

What they have discovered is that pollen is quite remarkable in what it contains for its size. Its vitamin content is substantial, including appreciable amounts of A, B_{12}, C, D, E and K, as well as thiamin, riboflavin, nicotinic acid, pantothenic acid, biotin, inositol, folic acid, lecithin, and rutin. The mineral content varies slightly according to the type of pollen and the soil in which the plant has grown, as we have seen, but the main minerals included in all pollen are iron, copper, sulphur, sodium, calcium, potassium, phosphorus, magnesium, manganese, and silicon. The average mineral content is something like 2.5 per cent of the grain, but because we only need to take fairly small amounts on a daily basis, pollen is a valuable supplement for mineral intake as well as vitamins.

The amino acid content of pollen is also high in comparison with its size – 10 per cent or more, and all the eight amino acids which the body cannot produce itself are included.

Pollen also contains enzymes, sugars, carbohydrates, and fats, so it has a very complete selection of nutrients which are as beneficial to man as they are to the bee.

POLLEN IN THE DIET

A daily supplement of pollen would be about 20g a day, taken in loose or tablet form. More would obviously be needed for anyone who was trying to relieve a specific ailment, or was run down, an invalid or elderly. It is best taken on an empty stomach – say, first thing in the morning, before breakfast. Anyone who is allergic to pollen should remember that airborne pollen is very different from that collected by the bee, in that the latter has been mixed with saliva and nectar, destroying the allergy-causing factor, so even hay-fever sufferers can take it.

Whilst researching into pollen generally, Swedish scientists discovered that they could extract the nucleus to make a product called Cernitin. Cernitin is made from the nuclei of pollen from flowers which have been organically grown for this specific purpose and can be bought in 30g or 60g tablets. It is even more concentrated than ordinary pollen grains, and is packed with vitamins, minerals, hormones, nucleic acid, and all of the amino acids. It is particularly good for colds, both as a preventative and as a cure. So there is a range of pollen products to choose from, as well as a blend of pollen and honey, which gives the advantages of both foods in one.

COMMERCIAL PRODUCTION OF POLLEN

Sweden, where all the pollen investigations began, is still really the home of the pollen industry, if it can be called that, not because the pollen is any different from that found elsewhere in the world, but because they have perfected the researching, planting and collecting expertise, and also the purifying of raw pollen so that no impurities remain. Although it is widely available in health food shops in the United Kingdom, and is produced there too, much of the world's pollen is imported from Sweden. The English climate is not normally conducive to large-scale production of honey or pollen, hence the import too of honeys from other countries, but the idea has caught on now that it is an important supplement, and though people in the UK did not know much about pollen or its uses until some ten years ago (when it was introduced to an English businessman in Sweden) no one can now deny the evidence that has been produced about it.

BENEFICIAL PROPERTIES

As well as being a good daily supplement, even for those in normal health, it will help in a range of illnesses, from the common cold already mentioned, to influenza, enteritis, constipation, urinary disorders, and anaemia. Because of its rutin content (and particularly so in wheat pollen since rutin is an ingredient of wheat germ) pollen strengthens the arteries and heart, and helps the blood to coagulate efficiently. Pollen is also an effective tonic for convalescents, particularly in the form of Cernitin tablets.

So here is another product of the hive, along with honey, propolis and royal jelly, that is equally beneficial to man. Like propolis, pollen has an antibiotic content and so acts as a destroyer of infection by bacteria, which is why it works with such things as colds by killing off the germs. Insomniacs have been helped by a course of pollen, and patients with nervous conditions have been soothed by its sedative and tonic effects. So even for someone who is apparently fit and well, here is a remarkable supplement – a tiny grain that is solid with the nutrients the body needs for good health and vitality.

CHAPTER ELEVEN

BRAN

Like wheat germ, bran is a part of the wheat grain that used to be automatically included in bread and all flour products, but is extracted from white flour today. It is the outer fibrous coating of the grain, and provides a fibre food or the essential roughage that we all need.

Bran accounts for about 19 per cent of the whole grain and is made up of five layers. Apart from being fibrous, these layers are all full of minerals, and beneath them is a layer called aleurone, which contains proteins and minerals. This material is husky and makes bread harder to chew, which is why it is extracted in the soft and tasteless white flour that goes into bread nowadays. But it also gives true wholewheat bread a delicious flavour and makes it a more satisfying thing to eat.

FLOUR WITHOUT BRAN

Flour is milled in various ways and with various results. Wholewheat flour contains all the wheat grain, whereas the flour known as 81 per cent, which is not as coarse as wholewheat, has had the bran removed and contains the endosperm and wheat germ. White flour, of course, contains nothing but the endosperm, or starch, with vitamins and minerals added to try and compensate for those that have been removed during milling and refining. White flour is made by a roller milling process which breaks down the grain into separate ingredients, so that the bran and so on can be extracted and the remaining starch ground even more finely into the soft white flour we know. Stone grinding is the method by which the grain is put between two circular millstones with cutting grooves on the face of each. The top stone revolves against the bottom one, and so the whole grain is ground at once and there is no chance of bits being extracted. To produce a slightly less coarse flour, the miller may sift out the bran and aleurone, or 19 per cent of the grain, leaving 81 per cent flour.

So if you always eat wholewheat bread anyway, you will naturally be getting the bran you need. You can also use bran separately in cooking and with cereals.

DIETARY FUNCTION

The main use of bran in nutrition is of course to activate the proper working of the intestines during digestion, and so avoid constipation, with which many people are afflicted and put up with because they can see no way round it. Refined food of today is bland and there is nothing in it to stimulate the activity of the large intestine and the descending colon, which processes waste matter from the body. As it builds up it becomes harder to eliminate and so chronic constipation occurs.

Far from being an irritant, as some people think, the fibre foods – bran; brown rice; whole grains such as barley, rye and millet; and raw vegetables – clear congestion of the colon and activate the peristaltic movements necessary for elimination.

Similarly, bran helps other colonic diseases such as diverticulitis, which is inflammation in the bowel; this illness has only been recorded since the turn of the century, when roller ground flour was first introduced. Colitis, or inflammation of the colon, is also caused by fibreless diets and can be helped by introducing bran and other fibre foods into meals. There are two sorts of colitis: mucous colitis, where diarrhoea and constipation alternate and digestion is uncomfortable; and ulcerative colitis, which, as the name suggests, means that the colon is inflamed with ulcers. Fibre should be introduced into the diet gradually where these conditions are present, and overeating should be stringently avoided.

Obesity often goes hand in hand with constipation and a poor diet, full of starchy and sweet foods and little else. Bran will alleviate the constipation and also help towards the balanced diet that overweight people need to turn to.

DIFFERENT FORMS

Bran can be bought in health food shops and normally comes in two forms, coarse flakes and finer powder. The coarser version is considered to be best for colonic function because it holds water more effectively. It also has less density in a dosage, therefore less carbohydrate will be absorbed if this type is taken, and a weight problem will not be created.

Bran bought loose like this can be sprinkled on cereal, or added to soups and other fluids. To start with, a fairly small amount should be taken – say, 2 teaspoonsful at breakfast-time and two later in the day – and the quantity gradually increased if constipation persists, and as the body gets used to a more fibre-filled diet.

If you find the thought of bran taken straight an unpalatable one, the best way to use it is in baking. Wholegrain flour, as has been mentioned, has plenty of bran in it, and if this is used for making bread, cakes, and so on, the daily intake of bran will probably be enough. There are bran cereals too, though you should choose one made from whole cereals and without the addition of white sugar.

OTHER FIBRE FOODS

Anyone who has a tendency to constipation, or a 'lazy bowel', would do well to look at the whole diet, and introduce more fibre foods generally into it. Bran is the most effective laxative food as such, but there are other fibre foods that can go into the diet to make a varied menu of the right sorts of food.

Grains

Grains have already been mentioned – that is, the whole grain rather than just the husk in the case of bran. Therefore, we have wheat, and also oats, corn, barley, rye, millet, and buckwheat. All of these have important nutrients in them as well as being fibre foods. Oats contain a good deal of calcium, for instance, whilst millet is rich in vitamins.

Brown Rice

Brown rice, on which the outer husk remains, is a good fibre food, too, though white rice, like white bread, has had everything but the starch removed. In fact, the very outer skin on brown rice has also been removed because this is not digestible, but the bran and aleurone layers remain. Wholegrain pasta is also made from wholegrain flour and so has the fibrous constituents.

Vegetables
For fibre food, always eat potatoes with the skins on, for this is where the fibrous content is – and indeed, most of the nutritional content of the potato is contained in or just below the skin. Other root vegetables, such as carrots and turnips, are fibre providers, too, though carrots are best eaten raw, and all root vegetables should be baked or cooked slowly rather than boiled at a tremendous rate, which seems to be the usual way of cooking vegetables and only succeeds in destroying all the goodness.

Green vegetables like cabbage are delicious raw in salads as well, and much better for you than the boiled version. Most green vegetables have fibre content, and so add roughage to the diet without any carbohydrate content and consequent weight additions. Many more vegetables can be added to salads than people realize, and as much variety as possible should be introduced to make the dish more interesting. The more vegetables that are eaten raw, the better.

Fruit
Similarly, fruit has a certain amount of fibre content, particularly apples, oranges, peaches, prunes, and pears. Fruit with seeds, such as raspberries, are also good roughage.

So, although bran is *the* fibre food, a good and varied diet can be worked out by those who have laxative problems – or even those who want to avoid getting them – which provides a high-fibre content as well as the accompanying nutrients contained in these foods.

CHAPTER TWELVE

LECITHIN

What is lecithin? Unlike the other foods mentioned in this book, it is not something that is easily recognizable, something that can be picked from the hedgerows or found in a beehive. It is a part of many foods, and indeed we cannot function properly without it.

THE FAT FIGHTER

Lecithin is an emulsifying agent, which enables oil and water to mix. It was first isolated from egg yolks in the nineteenth century, and used subsequently to produce things where it was necessary to blend a fatty constituent with a water one. This had happened naturally throughout time, of course, when certain ingredients containing the then unknown lecithin were mixed together, such as in cooking, but it was not until relatively recently that it was realized what nutritional and medicinal value lecithin had.

Lecithin is itself a fatty substance found in oil-bearing foods such as egg yolks, and the soya bean which has become the prime source of it these days. Yet although it is a fat, it is also known as the fat fighter, because it acts on excessive fats in the body, put there through a bad diet, and thus helps to prevent the build-up of cholesterol which causes hardening of the arteries and heart disease.

Today's diet tends to contain more fat than it should, though fat is essential to life in the right form. Usually though, it is taken in the form of hard saturated fats, such as butter and other animal fats which cause a build-up of cholesterol. In addition to this, the processing of modern foodstuffs, as we have seen, removes much of the original nutritional value, including the lecithin. Therefore an unbalanced situation occurs where the necessary lecithin is not present to burn up the cholesterol-forming fat and use it up in energy. For this reason, lecithin foods or a lecithin supplement are not only important to prevent heart disease and protect the heart and arteries, and also for burning up fat where it remains in the body instead of being converted into energy. If the diet is not right, the body cannot produce its own lecithin, which is manufactured in the liver and passed round the blood stream. When this happens, an actual deficiency occurs, and fats build up in the body.

SOURCES OF LECITHIN
Soya is the prime source of lecithin, but other vegetable oils contain it too, so long as they have not been refined. We already know about egg yolks, and other sources are whole cereals, nuts and liver. Wheat germ has lecithin in it, so wholewheat bread and flour will contain some too. But it is important to make sure that all the foods are unrefined and contain all their original

ingredients. It should also be borne in mind that vegetable sources of lecithin are better than egg yolks really, because the latter also contain cholesterol and can cause a build-up if eaten in large quantities. Therefore, although eggs are still an important source and are used in commercial products, the vegetable sources are more effective at reducing cholesterol levels as they come in unsaturated form.

Lecithin can also be isolated and sold in supplement form, either granular or oil, and when buying these, the contents should be checked for saturated and unsaturated fat content. Thus if you are not sure of getting enough lecithin from your diet, you can add granules to drinks or cereals, and it seems from tests made that granular lecithin from soya beans is the best form to take.

Fat is an essential part of the diet if taken in the right quantity, because it provides energy without bulk to the diet. This is because the energy from fat is released slowly into the body, and, as it also has a high calorie content, a little goes a long way. Also contained in fat are oil-soluble vitamins A, D, E, and K, and various other nutrients, which make it valuable in itself. However, a fact to be remembered is that, because energy from fat is released gradually, the fat is stored in the body until needed, where it acts as insulation against cold, and body padding. If taken in reasonable amounts it affords essential protection to the organs of the body, but if fat is consumed in large quantities, it will not disperse, but will continue to collect and pad out the body into obesity.

SATURATED AND UNSATURATED FATS

Fats come in two forms – saturated and unsaturated. The saturated fats are the animal fats which are hard, rather than liquid like oil. Animal fats are lard, butter, hard cheeses, hard margarine, meat fat, and eggs. In addition to the basic fats themselves, many foods contain saturated fat – for example, chocolate and pastries.

Unsaturated fats are the liquid oils and products from them, or they can be found in the original source of the oil, such as nuts. Unsaturated oils can come from sunflowers, safflower, olives, corn, soya, peanuts, and can be found in poultry. Soft margarines made from vegetable oil are also unsatured.

The main difference between the two types of fat is that the unsaturated ones increase the body's cholesterol level, whilst the unsaturated ones have no effect on it. Indeed, polyunsaturated fats actually help to decrease it. They are always soft fats and include the vegetable and fish oils, and margarine is also made in polyunsaturated form.

CHOLESTEROL – ITS DANGER AND USES
Lecithin, therefore, is a polyunsaturated fat, and is the most effective one in the diet for reducing the cholesterol level and breaking down fat. Most people, even if they try to use vegetable oils for cooking and so on, are bound to absorb some hard fat in the form of meat fat, cheese, and egg yolks. This can largely be dispensed with by using polyunsaturated margarines instead of butter, eating more poultry and fish than red meat, cutting the fat from meat, cutting down on eggs, not eating too much fried food, and never using lard for frying, and of course taking a daily dose of lecithin.

Not so many years ago, people happily ate rich yellow butter, hard cheese, large slabs of red meat dripping with fat, and the word cholesterol was unheard of. For this reason, it is sometimes taken to be a new fad, something new to talk about, without much foundation in fact. But the fact is that cholesterol, like everything else, is all right in a balanced amount and if energy is used up. It is our lifestyle today, as much as an excess of animal fat, that causes a build-up of cholesterol and consequent hardening of the arteries and heart failure. People, rather than walking or riding, go everywhere by car, they sit in offices all day, they eat large lunches and then carry on sitting in offices. In other words, they do little to burn up the store of fat being put into their bodies, normally in hard, saturated form. People who take plenty of exercise during their working hours are far less likely to suffer heart failure and weight problems than their deskbound counterparts.

Cholesterol has of course always been with us and was not a problem until it was allowed to build up, and unbalanced diets meant that lecithin was not taken in to break it down. As well as being found in foods, it is also manufactured by the body, but the intake of soft fats means that the cholesterol is softened and becomes manageable. In the form of animal fats, not broken down, it takes on a solid, waxy form. In the proper diet, the cholesterol produced by the body will be soluble and able to pass into the bloodstream, where it helps in the formation of new body cells. But because cholesterol is fat, it cannot mix with water and so cannot pass into the bloodstream unless it is emulsified into usable form by lecithin. If the cholesterol content outweighs the amount of lecithin being taken in to break it down, it will remain solid and stick in the arteries. As time passes, it builds up on the artery walls and blocks the channels, forming the condition known as arteriosclerosis. If the cholesterol is broken down into soluble form, of course, it passes through the arteries with no trouble and enters the cells.

So cholesterol, being part of the body's make-up, does have its uses if properly emulsified and not allowed to build up in the arteries. It helps to build up the cells of the body and the hormones, and is present in the bile acids of the liver, which are needed to absorb fats in the intestine. Here again, unless the cholesterol is balanced by lecithin, it forms gall stones.

Again, in its proper form – that is, emulsified by lecithin – cholesterol lubricates the arteries so that the blood being pumped through does not damage the artery walls. And as we have seen, it is this very function in unbalanced form that can cause such problems with too much cholesterol not properly treated, building up in the arteries. Yet, correctly treated, it is actually very beneficial to the body.

In addition to all this, cholesterol can be converted into vitamin D when you are lying in the sun, say, and this vitamin is of course an important one for strong bone formation.

OBESITY REMEDY
Another cause of heart disease is obesity, which puts a strain on the heart, particularly as it is normally coupled with lack of exercise and a cholesterol-forming diet. Lecithin, as we have seen, breaks down fatty food, but it also breaks down actual fat on the body, even though this is not formed entirely of fats. Indeed, much of the fat-forming food is carbohydrate, or starch, such as bread and potatoes. So, provided that you take up a good calorie-controlled diet, a supplement of lecithin will help to burn up the fact faster. It also stops fat forming deposits in one place, which in turn causes unsightly bulges. Lecithin keeps the fat moving round the body, using it up for energy which can be done far more easily when it is in the form of small particles.

Some people are fat because of water retention, causing the body to swell in just the same way as overeating does. Excess fluid is removed by a diuretic, and lecithin, amongst its other properties, is a natural diuretic that rids the body of excess fluid.

So these are some of the reasons why lecithin can be called the fat fighter. Although it is a supplement that will probably be new to many people, its importance is growing with the realization of what causes weight problems and heart failure, and that this is a method of cutting down the risks. Of course, any of the supplements mentioned in this book should be combined with a good diet that is not excessive in any department and contains a full complement of nutrients, and lecithin is no exception, for it will not be effective against a diet based on large amounts of hard fats that are never worked off, although it will still go a long way to breaking them down. But combined with a sensible diet, it is a valuable, and even vital, addition.

FURTHER READING

Honey: Natural Food and Healer
  Janet Bord
Hanssen's Complete Cider Vinegar
  Maurice Hanssen
About Yogurt
  P.E. Norris
Kelp for Better Health and Vitality
  Frank Wilson
About Wheat Germ
  P.E. Norris
About Comfrey
  G.J. Binding
About Molasses
  P.E. Norris
About Soyabeans
  G.J. Binding
About Garlic
  G.J. Binding
The Healing Power of Pollen
  Maurice Hanssen
Bran
  Ray Hill
Lecithin
  Paul Simons
How to Eat for Health
  Stanley Lief
Natural Beauty
  Carol Hunter
Vitamins: What They Are and Why We Need Them
  Carol Hunter
Minerals: What They Are and Why We Need Them
  Miriam Polunin
The Wholefood Lunch Box
  Janet Hunt

INDEX